W9-BNN-322

The Bariatric Foodie Guide to

Perfect Protein Drinks

© Bariatric Foodie, 2012

Table of Contents

You CAN make delicious protein shakes!

Yes you. The one with this book in your hands trying to decide whether to invest money in a protein shake recipe book when you've hated EVERY protein shake you've ever tasted. Yep, you can make a delicious protein shake.

And you too…the person holding this book wondering if you should invest in a protein shake recipe book when you have a default shake you *like*…it's just that it's gotten a bit old. You too can "shake it up" and make new and delicious protein shakes.

And I'm going to show you how.

But what makes me so qualified to do this? I mean, who died and made *me* Queen of the Protein Shakes? Why should you even trust that you'll like any of the protein shake recipes in this book?

That's a good question. I'd be asking it myself if I were about to fork over money for a protein shake book.
Here's what makes *this* protein shake book different.

Wait…I'm getting ahead of myself. First off, hi! I'm Nikki. I am several years out from roux-en-y gastric bypass surgery and lost a total of 155 lbs.

And because I know that assertion only means so much in the weight loss surgery world, I'll wait a moment while you check out my awesome back cover photo. See the collar bones?

There? Convinced now? Good!

My experience with protein shakes goes back to my very first days after surgery. My mother made my first shake out of chocolate whey powder and milk…and nothing else. You can imagine how that went. But those early horrific days had a purpose! The small amounts I could eat dictated that I come to terms with protein shakes. My hatred of protein shakes dictated that I experiment. The combination of these two factors culminated in this glorious work you are holding in your hands and are becoming increasingly convinced you *should* in fact buy.

Through my adventures in cooking and protein shake making, I started a blog called "Bariatric Foodie," (www.bariatricfoodie.com), a little place to share my recipes just in case they helped anyone. From there a lot of stuff happened but I won't bore you with the details. The most significant thing that happened is that I adopted a philosophy for the way I relate my recipes to the weight loss surgery community. Play with your food.

"Play with your food?"

Yep…that's right. Since we can't eat as much food…and our tastes change…and we have very specific nutrition requirements, I started a advocating for people to play with their food. Now this isn't a completely radical idea. The nature of recipes sort of lends itself to experimentation. But really, how many recipes do you read that encourage you to put your unique spin on them? And how many cooks implore you to not only share but celebrate how you changed their recipe?

Which brings me back to why this book is unique. At this point I envision you're short on time, so I'll try to be brief.

Part of playing with your food is knowing how food works. Yes, that includes protein shakes. What makes them thick? What makes them thin? What makes them foamy? What makes them sweet or bitter or funky smelling?

You need to know these things so you can make shakes the way you want them. In short, I can give you all the recipes in the world, but if you hate foamy, overly sweet protein shakes, the way I wrote the recipe may leave you with an even more intense hatred of them.

So yes…I do give you recipes but I also give you some insight into what makes protein shakes taste the way they do and how to produce certain flavors and textures according to your likes and dislikes. I even give you some tools to experiment and invent your own protein shakes.

Wow. That's a lot of stuff, huh?

So if you're wondering if you'll like the recipes in this book...my answer is you really don't have to. Instead, you need only a mind adventurous enough to consider the recipes I've given and how they can help you come up with ideas for *your* own recipes. And I give you everything you need to be able to take those ideas to the next level.

Now...this is do-or-die time. If I've entertained you up to this point...you should see what's beyond this page!

I trust you'll make the right decision. See you on the other side.

Protein Drinks 101

Like I said in the introduction to this book, it's not really necessary to fall in love with *my* recipes to have a great protein shake experience. But to transform your protein shake experiences you do, however, need a few key pieces of information:

1. You need to know what you like in terms of textures, flavors and consistency.

2. You need to know what protein shakes are made of.

3. You need to know how those components work together to create various textures, flavors and consistencies.

Learn those three things and *nothing* can stop you from finding a protein drink that you like (or at least can tolerate). In this section, we're going to learn about these things so that when you move on to the next section (the one with the recipes!) you'll have a good idea of how you'll approach your protein drinks.

So let's start at the beginning, shall we?

Protein Shake Personality Quiz

Part of having a blissful shake experience is having a clear idea of what you absolutely do and do not like. Take this short quiz to find out YOUR protein shake personality.

Before surgery (or now if you are pre-op), my snack food of choice was:

   a)   Salty and crunchy

   b)   Sweet and chewy

My favorite type of frozen drink is:

   a)   A milkshake

   b)   A fruit smoothie

   c)   A Slurpee

   d)   Frappucino

If you like milk shakes, you liked them:

   a)   Triple thick: so thick you could turn the cup over and the shake wouldn't fall out!

   b)   Fairly thick but not solid

   c)   Fairly thin

Post-op, when you want something to drink, are you are more likely to reach for a:

   a)   Cup of hot coffee or tea

   b)   A tall glass of ice water, tea or drink mix

When making yourself a drink post-op do you find yourself:

   a)   Adding sweetener to get it to a taste you like

   b)   Leaving it plain or with the amount of sweetener it already contains

   c)   Everything tastes too sweet, so you generally drink water

Question 1: if you answered "a" you might consider adding unflavored protein to savory foods. While they, in and of themselves, don't provide crunch, you can add that easily as your eating stage allows. If you answered "b" you will probably do well with a protein shake!

Question 2: if you answered (a) traditional protein shake recipes with a milk base will probably serve you well. If you answered (b) you might want to start with the fruity drink recipes in this book and use a water/frozen fruit base. If you answered (c) you would do well to combine sugar-free drink sticks with unflavored protein, water and ice (there's a tutorial later in this section). If you answered (d) you might want to start with the "coffeehouse knock-off" recipes and use decaffeinated coffee as your shake base.

Question 3: if you answered (a) pay close attention to the tutorial on the "Triple X" method for mixing a protein shake. If you answered (b) you might use the Triple X method with a bit less ice than I call for in the tutorial. If you answered (c) you might want to either make your shake in a shaker cup or without ice at all.

Question 4: If you answered (a) you'll probably want to check out my "how to make a hot protein drink" tutorial. If you answered (b) you're good to go with (almost) every recipe in this book!

Question 5: If you answered (a) make sure to invest in a good no-calorie sweetener. But don't go overboard! If you answered (b) it might be best to simply use the sugar free syrups in the recipes but no additional sweetener. If you answered (c) again, you can also add unflavored protein to your savory foods like soup, using the hot mixing method in this book.

The Anatomy of a (Good) Protein Drink

Now that you know what you like, how do you make your protein shake conform? First, you need a crash course on the inner workings of a protein shake.

All protein drinks are made up of four things: the base, the protein powder, flavor additives and texture additives. I've had folks propose other parts of a shake but they usually all fit into those four broad categories. Let's explore each one.

The Base

That's just an official sounding term for whatever liquid or semi-liquid substance you use to make your protein drink. For some, that would be water, for others milk, for others still yogurt. The choice is truly yours.

For those who like creamy, milkshake-style drinks, milk of some sort is your best base option. There are many different kinds of milk and the kind you choose depends on your particular situation. For most people, cow's milk seems the default option. Even within cow's milk there are decisions to be made, such as what level of milk fat you'll use.

While that is a truly personal decision, I will say that fat-free (skim) milk has 80 calories, 12 grams of carbohydrates and 8 grams of protein. Some post-ops fret about the carbohydrates in cow's milk. You really need not. Those carbohydrates work with the fat and protein to give you energy, among other things. But the carb count on cow's milk does mean that you might want to watch any additional carbs you add to your shake. Remember, a protein shake should be *protein* forward.

Many roux-en-y gastric bypass post-ops in particular find themselves lactose intolerant after surgery. For them, standard cow's milk is not an option. Thankfully there are a plethora of options. There is cow's milk designed for those who are lactose intolerant, which adds lactase (the enzyme that isn't produced by lactose intolerant systems). There's also soy milk, rice milk and almond milk. All bring a different set of characteristics to the table. When considering which milk to use as a base, might I suggest using the "Your Protein Drink Test Kitchen" tool at the end of the book to work out what's best for you.

For those who aren't into the creamy thing, and specifically those who are instead into the fruity thing, water is a good base option. Water won't give you the protein of milk, of course, but it does still have its own benefits. Namely, water! Adults need at least 64 ounces of water a day to maintain optimum health, but after weight loss surgery, especially in the beginning, that can be difficult. "Multi-tasking" can help. Meeting your fluid needs at the same time as your protein needs can be a great help, especially in the days and weeks after surgery.

To be fair, both milk and water count toward your fluid intake for the day, but if you don't like milky shakes, take heart — you're still doing a good thing for yourself!

For smoothies, yogurt serves as a good base for your protein drink. Because yogurt is thick, in most commercial blenders, you need at least a little bit of liquid to blend the shake. If so, it's your choice — milk or water.

The Protein

I'll go more in depth about choosing the right protein powder later. For now you need to just remember one thing (and I'll repeat it enough times that by the end of this book you'll remember it). Protein is only *one* ingredient in your protein drink. It is not *the* drink. That means that even if you don't particularly care for the powder itself, it is possible to make a drink that you like.

Flavor Additives

Here's where we get to the fun part. Flavor additives can make or break your protein drink. Add the right ones and you can go from hell to heaven in a matter of seconds. The wrong one can ruin your whole day. That's why it's important to be careful about flavor additives. Once you find something you like, stay within that family of flavors and explore until you feel adventurous again. Or…be like me and just go into it full throttle.

But there is a danger to flavor additives. Many have calories. And those calories may or may not be beneficial. Protein shakes should be protein forward. People have sent me their shake recipes in the past, not knowing that their flavor additives actually tipped the balance of nutrients so that their shake had actually ceased to be a *protein* shake and ventured into that dangerous territory called "a carbohydrate with a decent protein count." You don't want to be in that place. It's not pretty.

You also don't want to add things to your shake that give you way too many calories for the amount of protein you're getting back. The most common example of this is peanut butter. Now, don't get me wrong. I LOVE the stuff. Any of you who know me online know I love the stuff. But I will never, ever put it in my protein shake. Why? A tablespoon is nearly 100 calories but only gives me 3.5 grams of protein in return! To me, that's about as ridiculous as paying $100 for something worth $3.50.

That's not to say all additives *have* to have great protein counts. You just need to consider the whole picture. Bottom line: my personal rule is this. Additives typically don't make up more than 50 calories in my shake unless those calories give me a good amount of protein. What's a good amount of protein? I consider a food to have a good amount of protein if there is one gram of protein for every ten calories. If it's over 50 calories, it needs to meet that threshold. Otherwise, it's out!

But within that rule, there are lots of things I can afford to put in my shake that aren't particularly protein heavy that give me other benefits, namely:

- ½ c. frozen berries (various micro-nutrients along with fiber)

- ½ banana (potassium, fiber)

- Peanut flour (good fat and protein)

These are just a few examples. You'll see others in my recipes.

I also use zero calorie flavor additives. Sugar substitute is the most common one. This is another personal decision you'll have to make. Some people swear by sucralose (Splenda), aspartame (Sweet 'n Low) or Nutri-Sweet (Equal). Others are sensitive to artificial sweeteners and instead go with Stevia or fructose.

I would like to clear up one common misconception about sucralose in particular. Many nutritionists tell their clients not to use it because it has calories and carbs. This is true…*kinda*. Yes, sucralose does have carbs in it. In and of itself, sucralose is so lightweight that without some starch it'd just fly away. Thankfully the amount starch in a teaspoon of sucralose is so minimal that the calories can't be measured. As for the sucralose itself, our bodies can't absorb it so it doesn't count as ingested calories.

What does this all mean to you? If you are making a recipe with a boatload of sucralose (and I sometimes do), you might want to check your handy calorie counter because in large quantities it does have a calorie and carb count. For one or two packets, it's negligible and I wouldn't worry about it. Again, that's a personal choice.

The last type of flavoring agent I'd like to talk about is sugar-free syrups and extracts. When I reference sugar-free syrups in my recipes, I'm not talking about the kind like a pancake or ice cream sundae syrup. I'm actually speaking of the type of syrups used at coffeehouses to flavor your favorite coffee drinks. These syrups are typically zero calories and come in a variety of flavors. See the resource section for more information.

Texture Additives

Texture additives are things you add to your shake to elicit the kind of consistency that you like. Usually, texture additives are used in either protein desserts (which we won't cover extensively in this book) or cold protein shakes and they are usually used to make cold shakes creamy.

To the naked eye, a texture additive might seem like it should be a flavor additive. In some cases it does double-duty. Take sugar-free pudding mix, for example. When added in small quantities to a protein shake, it lends itself to a creamier, thicker shake like one you'd get at your favorite ice cream shop.

You'll notice, however, that in my recipes even when there is pudding mix used, I also use some sort of flavor additive. Why? Portion control! A one tablespoon serving of sugar-free pudding mix is about 40 calories but doesn't give you any protein (only a few carbohydrates). Great additive, right? The problem is, the flavor you want doesn't always come through with just that one tablespoon. Adding more tips the balance of nutrients in your shake. So, I usually use pudding mix along with a no-calorie flavor additive, like zero calorie flavored syrup.

Other texture additives include unflavored gelatin and ice. If you don't like cold shakes at all, you don't really have to worry much about texture additives, but if you do, my personal rules for them are the same as flavor additives: under 50 calories and it can get away with not having a great protein count If it has some other benefit (in this case, I view the ability to make my protein shake into a milkshake a benefit). If not, reconsider it. If it's over 50 calories, look for that protein!

Now all this is a moot point if you're fine with just your protein powder and base by itself. Most protein powders contain flavor and texture additives of their own that are built into the calorie counts you see on the nutrition label. If you like your powder and base as-is, don't fix what's not broken. If you can barely stand the two together, start playing with your food! To start, I suggest using the "Your Protein Drink Test Kitchen" tool to work out your own unique recipe.

So with the anatomy of a protein shake in hand...let us now move on to the next challenge: mixing! And I'm not talking about the kind you do when you're a DJ!

Mixing Protein Drinks

How you mix your protein drink will ultimately determine its texture and, of course, is a big part of whether you love it or hate it. So let's go over the various ways you can mix protein to get to different consistencies.

Hot Protein Drinks

If you ask ten different post-ops who make hot protein drinks how they do it, you'll likely get ten different answers. This answer is just one of many and if there is a way you've found works better for you, I say go for it!

Before we get to the method, let's talk about what will happen if you simply add boiling hot water to your protein powder. It's a horrid experience, really, and I hope by writing this I'll spare you from ever having it. But when you simply add hot water to a protein powder, the powder curdles. You get large balls that we, in the weight loss surgery community have termed "floaties."

Floaties don't dissolve into the hot water and their consistency is rubbery. If you have the misfortune to ingest a floatie, you get the brunt of the intense protein flavor of the powder. And it's just plain disgusting.

Myth: Heating protein powder destroys the protein within

Some people will tell you that you destroy the nutritional content of protein powder by heating it past a certain temperature (130 degrees seems to be the common adage). <u>This is not true</u>.

In both how it behaves in reaction to heat and in nutritional content, think of protein powder kind of like an egg. Anyone who's ever made custard knows the importance of slowly raising the temperature of an egg (also called "tempering" an egg) so that it doesn't scramble in the hot liquid. The same is true with protein powder. Quickly combining protein powder with hot liquid will cause it to cook. Slowly bringing the temperature up will allow it to blend.

Also, when you cook an egg, you take it from one state of being to another. But in cooking an egg, it does not cease to be a source of protein. While it is true that the structure of the egg has changed – the whites and the yolk harden – the egg still contains the protein that it had when it was inside the shell. The same is true for protein powder. The form of the powder changes (in cold drinks, protein powder pretty much stays intact, it just blends in well with milk and ice. If you don't believe me, let your protein drink sit in room temperature for about 20 minutes. It will separate, leaving a layer of milk and flavoring and a layer of protein powder) but it's still a good protein source.

The Bariatric Foodie™ Method to Making Perfect Hot Protein Drinks

Here's how I make my hot protein drinks. Again, you may have heard of other ways and you may even be using some other ways. If so, you are welcome to use whatever method suits you!

1. In a cup or mug, combine equal parts protein powder and <u>room temperature</u> (not cold) liquid. This could be water or milk. You may also add other dry ingredients you plan to use in your drink (i.e. instant coffee or cocoa powder). Don't add dry nondairy creamer yet. Add that with your flavorings at the end.

2. Stir until a thick paste (sludge-like) develops.

3. <u>Slowly</u> fill the cup 1/3 of the way full with boiling hot water and stir your mixture until the water is incorporated. Stir it a bit more.

4. Repeat this process with the second 1/3 and the third 1/3 until your cup or mug is full, stopping each time to stir and incorporate your liquid.

5. Proceed with adding any flavorings you wish to add.

It may take some practice, but eventually you should be able to make a hot protein drink that is lump-free!

Cold Protein Drinks

I know what you're thinking. "I'm not an idiot! I know how to use a blender!" Well making a *good* shake sometimes takes a bit of technique. For instance, here's a method I developed of mixing cold shakes that deals with that nasty foam we all hate.

The Triple X Method for Mixing Protein Shakes

When I first started making protein shakes, I made them fairly thin, mostly because I didn't know how *not* to make them that way. But I didn't like the consistency of thin shakes for several reasons.

First, the foam that develops as a result of mixing protein powder and water was extremely bothersome to me. Having to get through that foam to my shake was challenging. Also, I have always been a triple thick girl. I believe a large part of this process is perception. If I perceived myself drinking a triple thick shake, especially in the beginning when I didn't want to eat *anything*, then it was a much more pleasant experience all around.

The Triple X method utilizes the foam that develops in protein shakes to create a thick, frothy drink. Here's how you do it:

Step 1: Combine your dry ingredients (protein powder, pudding mix, etc.) and your wet ingredients (milk, sugar-free syrup, etc.) in a blender and blend on a medium speed (if your blender has a "milkshake" setting that would be the proper speed) for two minutes.

Step 2: Before the liquid has a chance to settle, add enough ice so that approximately two ice cubes break the surface of the liquid (the number of cubes will vary by how much liquid you use).

Step 3: Blend again (on Frappe or ice crushing setting) for another 1- 2 minutes or until you can no longer hear ice breaking in the blender.

Step 4: Pour and enjoy!

Why does this work? Well, I'm not a scientist so I can only offer a theory.

Blending the shake for a full two minutes makes it very aerated, a fact that is quite bothersome in a thinner shake. Then, when you add ice and blend at an even higher speed, you are quickly crushing the ice, mixing the froth in and cooling the whole thing down at the same time.

In the end, it doesn't matter to me *why* it works. I'm much more concerned that it *does* actually work. And, if "field reports" from Bariatric Foodie fans are any indicator, when done correctly, the Triple X method DOES work!

A few warnings:

- Triple X shakes, made according to the recipes in this book, are BIG. If you can't drink that much, consider halving or even quartering the recipe.

- If you use a very large blender, you might not achieve the "two ice cubes breaking the surface" rule. In those cases, I'd recommend 5-6 ice cubes.

- Just like any other cold protein shake, if you allow it to sit too long, it will separate. If you know you'll be sipping on it a while, transfer it into a blender cup so you can re-mix it as necessary

Not only does the Triple X method give you a thick, creamy shake, it also gives you a lot of additional water (a challenge for many post-ops). Consider this: 1 ice cube = 1 oz. of water. So you're adding to your water totals by using this method!

Protein Frozen Treats

Let's face it…we got our digestive systems operated on, not our heads. So sometimes we still want a sweet treat…and not of the protein shake variety.

I like ice cream. Who doesn't? That's why I was so excited to see, on a popular weight loss surgery food blog, a recipe for protein ice cream. But I was dubious at first: would it really taste good? I mean…*really?*

So I gave it a try. And I learned a few things, which I am about to share with you. By using these tips, many of the recipes in this book can be made into a protein frozen treat.

Protein Ice Cream

Traditional ice cream is a frozen custard. While protein ice cream *can* be made that way, the quickest way to make it is to make it from a protein shake base. Here's how to do it:

1. Make a double portion of any of the recipes in this book. Be sure all your ingredients (protein powder, additional flavoring ingredients) are in this. It will serve as your ice cream base.

2. Be sure to add a bit of additional no-calorie sweetener to your ice

cream base. A general cooking rule of thumb: heating something with sweetener intensifies sweetness, chilling something with sweetener dulls the sweetness. It will take a few tries to find your particular sweetness threshold.

3. Make sure your shake is VERY aerated (make the ice cream base as if you were making a Triple X protein shake). This will help it to remain creamy as it chills in the ice cream maker.

4. This may seem like a no-brainer, but I cannot count how many times I've heard of people making this mistake: make sure the cylinder to your ice cream maker is frozen solid before putting it into your ice cream maker!

5. Add your ice cream base to your ice cream maker and turn it on. Let it churn for about 15-20 minutes or until it begins to set.

6. If you are using any "chunky additives" (I suggest some in various shake recipes), add them and allow the ice cream to churn an additional 5-7 minutes.

At this point you'll have a soft-serve like ice cream. If you like that consistency, dig in! If you want a scoop of ice cream, transfer the ice cream to a storage container and put it in the freezer for about an hour.

Some tips/warnings:

- Don't use skim milk to make protein ice cream. Ice cream needs a little bit of fat to be decadent. If you want to save on calories, use 1% milk, but I'd suggest 2% if possible.

- Because you are making homemade ice cream, when you store it in the freezer, it's going to freeze solid. When you want more ice cream, you can just sit your storage container on the kitchen counter for about 10 minutes before you plan to eat it.

Protein Gelato

This is actually a misnomer, but it's the best term to describe the final product. Protein gelato is a lot like protein ice cream, except it is thicker and creamier. Here's how you make it.

1. Combine protein powder and flavoring ingredients with an entire box of pudding (in a complimentary flavor, i.e. chocolate pudding

with chocolate ice cream, etc.)

2. Instead of using two cups of milk, use three (this prevents the pudding from completely setting).

3. Since the pudding mix has additional sweetener, taste the base before deciding to add additional no-calorie sweetener. A good base should taste just slightly too sweet. If it is sickeningly sweet, it will be too sweet in cold form.

4. Add your gelato base to the ice cream maker and follow instructions 5-6 from protein ice cream.

Protein Sorbet

Protein sorbet is made a lot like traditional sorbet. Unlike traditional ice cream bases, sorbet doesn't require the tempering of eggs. You can use any of the shakes in the "fruity shakes" section to make a protein sorbet, by using the following process:

1. Combine ½ c. water with a ½ cup Splenda and bring to a boil (bump up to a full cup if you like really sweet sorbet). This is called sugar-free simple syrup. TIP: if you want to take your sorbet to the next level, add a few mint leaves to the water when making the simple syrup.

2. Make a double portion of your shake, except instead of using the liquid called for in the shake, use the simple syrup. Add more water as necessary to create a smoothie consistency.

3. Don't skip the lemon juice! Sorbet gets its tart flavor from the lemon juice.

4. Add the sorbet base to ice cream maker and follow steps 5-6 from protein ice cream.

5. Freeze in a container for about 30 minutes before eating so that you can scoop it.

Protein Popsicles

Protein popsicles are very refreshing in the summertime. They can be made from either a protein ice cream, gelato or sorbet recipe. All that is required is a set of popsicle molds.

A few pieces of advice:

- Only make a single portion of shake as a base or else you'll have more popsicle base than popsicle molds to hold it!

- After freezing, if you can't automatically get your popsicle out of the base, run the mold under room temperature water for a few moments to loosen it up.

So now that you're all educated on what makes a great protein shake and how to mix a great protein treat, let's get to the fun part—recipes!

Protein Shake Recipes

How to Use the Recipes

Each protein shake recipe given can serve a number of purposes. In addition to making cold shakes, many of the recipes can be used to make hot drinks and frozen treats.

For shakes that work best only as hot or cold versions, I've only given the directions for that variation (although you are certainly welcome to make it any way you like). Nearly all shakes can be used to make frozen treats. Remember, water-based shakes will come out like sorbet while milk based shakes will come out like ice cream.

Some recipes call for specialty purchases. I give more information on specialty purchases in the Resources section, but I also try give alternatives to the special purchase that can be found in most grocery stores.

What you won't find in this book

It may seem highly unusual, but I don't include nutrition information for my shakes and that is for a good reason. There is a great variation between the products that are available to each of us. Further, you may decide to make tweaks to the recipe to make it more to your liking (which is perfectly fine. I love when people play with their food!).

All this being the case, I leave it to you to figure out the nutritional information (I commonly call these the "stats" for a recipe) for yourself. But don't fret! The "Your Protein Shake Test Kitchen" tool at the back of the book gives you everything you need to figure out the nutrition information for the shake you make your own.

Unfortunately there's also no pictures! Sorry, but pictures are expensive and I want everyone to be able to afford shake joy! But there are plenty of shake photos on Bariatric Foodie!

This is not the end!

While I've compiled an extensive list of great protein shakes here, I'm continually playing with my recipes and coming up with new ones. Check Bariatric Foodie (bariatricfoodie.com) to see what's shaking!

Those shake recipes are the base for almost every shake recipe listed. If you are a person who doesn't like a lot of flavor combinations, you could easily stick to one of these and be fine!

Basic Chocolate

8 oz. milk

1 scoop chocolate protein powder

1 tbsp. no-calorie, sugar-free chocolate syrup

1 tbsp. sugar-free, fat-free chocolate pudding mix

Bonus tips:

To amp up the chocolate flavor in any recipe, add 1 tsp. of instant decaffeinated coffee. You'll never taste the coffee—only the intensified chocolate flavor!

Also the no-calorie sugar-free syrups referenced are like those used in coffeehouses. Torani and DaVinci are two popular brand names.

Basic Vanilla

8 oz. milk

1 scoop vanilla protein powder

1 tbsp no-calorie, sugar-free vanilla syrup

1 tbsp sugar-free, fat-free vanilla pudding mix

Basic Strawberry

8 oz. milk

1 scoop strawberry protein powder

½ cup fresh or frozen strawberries

1 tbsp no-calorie sweetener

Classic Dessert Shakes

These shakes taste like your favorite desserts from your pre-op life!

Bananas foster

Anyone who has had this wonderful, warm treat can attest to its ability to calm even the most raging sweet tooth.

8 oz. milk

1 scoop vanilla protein powder

1 tbsp. sugar-free, fat-free banana cream pudding mix

1 tbsp. sugar-free caramel syrup

1 tbsp. sugar-free butter rum syrup

> **Swap:**
>
> Instead of the Butter Rum sugar free syrup, use 1/8 tsp. of Rum Extract.

To make a cold shake:

1. Combine all dry ingredients with milk and syrup in a blender

2. For a thicker shake, blend for two minutes. For a thinner shake, blend for one minute.

3. For a thinner shake, allow liquid to settle before transferring to a glass.

4. For a thicker shake, add 5-6 cubes of ice and blend until all ice is crushed.

To make a hot drink:

1. Heat milk in microwave until hot (about 30-45 seconds)

2. Combine dry ingredients (including sweetener) in a 12 oz. mug with 4 oz. room temperature water and stir until a thick paste develops.

3. Slowly add hot milk to paste mixture while stirring vigorously.

4. If mixture isn't warm enough, heat in microwave for an additional 30 seconds.

5. Add syrups to the hot mixture.

German Chocolate Cake

I know, I know…there are some foods where the enjoyment comes just as much from the texture as from the flavor…but you can't have German chocolate cake right now! So drink this!

8 oz milk

1 scoop chocolate protein powder

2 tbsp sugar-free German chocolate cake syrup

1 tbsp unsweetened cocoa powder

3 packets no-calorie sweetener (or to taste)

Swaps:

In the absence of German chocolate cake flavored syrup, add 1 tbsp. each chocolate, either English Toffee or Caramel, and toasted coconut SF syrups.

In the absence of any sugar-free syrup, add one drop coconut extract and 1 tbsp. sugar-free caramel coffee creamer.

To make a cold shake:

1. Combine all dry ingredients with milk and syrup in a blender

2. For a thicker shake, blend for two minutes. For a thinner shake, blend for one minute.

3. For a thinner shake, allow liquid to settle before transferring to a glass.

4. For a thicker shake, add 5-6 cubes of ice and blend until all ice is crushed.

To make a hot drink:

1. Heat milk in microwave until hot (about 30-45 seconds)

2. Combine dry ingredients (including sweetener) in a 12 oz. mug with 4 oz. room temperature water and stir until a thick paste develops.

3. Slowly add hot milk to paste mixture while stirring vigorously.

4. If mixture isn't warm enough, heat in microwave for an additional 30 seconds.

5. Add syrup to the hot mixture.

30

Banana bread

I have it on good authority that this really does taste like banana bread. I think so too but sometimes I have to do "independent taste tests" to ensure I'm giving folks accurate depictions!

8 oz milk

1 scoop vanilla protein powder

1 tbsp sugar-free, fat-free banana cream pudding mix

> **Tip:**
>
> Top with a bit of fat free whipped cream and just a few toasted walnut pieces to get the full effect!

2 tbsp sugar-free pumpkin pie syrup (or 1/8 tsp. pumpkin pie spice)

3 packets of no-calorie sweetener (or to taste)

1 drop of butter extract

To make a cold shake:

1. Combine all dry ingredients with milk, syrup and extract in a blender

2. For a thicker shake, blend for two minutes. For a thinner shake, blend for one minute.

3. For a thinner shake, allow liquid to settle before transferring to a glass.

4. For a thicker shake, add 5-6 cubes of ice and blend until all ice is crushed.

To make a hot drink:

1. Heat milk in microwave until hot (about 30-45 seconds)

2. Combine dry ingredients (including sweetener) in a 12 oz. mug with 4 oz. room temperature water and stir until a thick paste develops.

3. Slowly add hot milk to paste mixture while stirring vigorously.

4. If mixture isn't warm enough, heat in microwave for an additional 30 seconds.

5. Add extract and syrup to hot liquid.

Apple Pie

What could be more American than apple pie? I use sugar-free apple cider mix here because it already has the same spices you'd find in apple pie.

8 oz. milk

1 scoop vanilla protein powder

1 packet sugar-free apple cider mix

1 tbsp. no-calorie sweetener

1/8 tsp. butter extract

> **Swap:**
>
> If you can't find sugar-free apple cider mix, you can substitute 1/4 c no-sugar added apple sauce + 1/8 tsp. apple pie spice.

To make a cold shake:

1. Combine all dry ingredients with milk and extract in a blender

2. For a thicker shake, blend for two minutes. For a thinner shake, blend for one minute.

3. For a thinner shake, allow liquid to settle before transferring to a glass.

4. For a thicker shake, add 5-6 cubes of ice and blend until all ice is crushed.

To make a hot drink:

1. Heat milk in microwave until hot (about 30-45 seconds).

2. Combine dry ingredients (including sweetener) in a 12 oz. mug with 4 oz. room temperature water and stir until a thick paste develops.

3. Slowly add hot milk to paste mixture while stirring vigorously.

4. If mixture isn't warm enough, heat in microwave for an additional 30 seconds.

5. Add extract to the hot mixture.

Nutella

Folks in the U.S. are JUST starting to latch on to the yumminess that is Nutella. If you are one of them, you'll love this shake!

8 oz. milk
1 scoop chocolate protein powder
1 tbsp. dry sugar-free, fat free chocolate pudding mix
1 tsp. good instant decaf coffee
4-5 pumps sugar-free hazelnut syrup

To make a cold shake:

1. Combine all dry ingredients with milk and syrup in a blender.

2. For a thicker shake, blend for two minutes. For a thinner shake, blend for one minute.

3. For a thinner shake, allow liquid to settle before transferring to a glass.

4. For a thicker shake, add 5-6 cubes of ice and blend until all ice is crushed.

To make a hot drink:

1. Heat milk in microwave until hot (about 30-45 seconds).

2. Combine dry ingredients in a 12 oz. mug with 4 oz. room temperature water and stir until a thick paste develops.

3. Slowly add hot milk to paste mixture while stirring vigorously.

4. If mixture isn't warm enough, heat in microwave for an additional 30 seconds.

5. Add syrup to the hot mixture.

Cinnabun

Sadly the original version of this crave-worthy dessert is probably doomed to our "extreme moderation list" for life. In such situations, there's only one thing to do...reinvent! I should note, I much prefer this as a hot drink than a cold one.

8 oz. milk

1 scoop vanilla protein powder

1 tbsp. sugar-free, fat-free cheesecake pudding mix

1 tbsp. sugar-free cinnamon syrup

1/8 tsp. butter extract

To make a cold shake:

1. Combine all dry ingredients with milk, syrup and extract in a blender.

2. For a thicker shake, blend for two minutes. For a thinner shake, blend for one minute.

3. For a thinner shake, allow liquid to settle before transferring to a glass.

4. For a thicker shake, add 5-6 cubes of ice and blend until all ice is crushed.

To make a hot drink:

1. Heat milk in microwave until hot (about 30-45 seconds).

2. Combine dry ingredients (including sweetener) in a 12 oz. mug with 4 oz. room temperature water and stir until a thick paste develops.

3. Slowly add hot milk to paste mixture while stirring vigorously.

4. If mixture isn't warm enough, heat in microwave for an additional 30 seconds.

5. Add extract and syrup to hot mixture.

Cheesecake Shakes

These shakes take all the flavor of the rich, decadent dessert you love and leave many of the calories and grams of fat behind.

Strawberry Cheesecake

If you get just the right amount of ice cubes in there, this smooth, creamy drink even FEELS like the real thing!

8 oz. milk

1 scoop strawberry protein powder

1 tbsp. sugar-free, fat-free cheesecake pudding mix

2 tbsp. sugar-free vanilla syrup

½ tsp. lemon juice OR 1 packet of True Lemon

3 packets no-calorie sweetener (or to taste).

To make a cold shake:

1. Combine all dry ingredients with milk and syrup in a blender.

2. For a thicker shake, blend for two minutes. For a thinner shake, blend for one minute.

3. For a thinner shake, allow liquid to settle before transferring to a glass.

4. For a thicker shake, add 5-6 cubes of ice and blend until all ice is crushed.

To make a hot drink:

1. Heat milk in microwave until hot (about 30-45 seconds).

2. Combine dry ingredients (including sweetener) in a 12 oz. mug with 4 oz. room temperature water and stir until a thick paste develops.

3. Slowly add hot milk to paste mixture while stirring vigorously.

4. If mixture isn't warm enough, heat in microwave for an additional 30 seconds.

5. Add syrup to hot mixture.

Cherry Cheesecake

8 oz. milk

1 scoop vanilla protein powder

1 tbsp. sugar-free, fat-free cheesecake pudding mix

1 tbsp. sugar-free cherry (or black cherry) syrup

½ tsp. lemon juice OR 1 packet True Lemon

3 packets no-calorie sweetener (or to taste)

To make a cold shake:

1. Combine all dry ingredients with milk and syrup in a blender.

2. For a thicker shake, blend for two minutes. For a thinner shake, blend for one minute.

3. For a thinner shake, allow liquid to settle before transferring to a glass.

4. For a thicker shake, add 5-6 cubes of ice and blend until all ice is crushed.

To make a hot drink:

1. Heat milk in microwave until hot (about 30-45 seconds).

2. Combine dry ingredients (including sweetener) in a 12 oz. mug with 4 oz. room temperature water and stir until a thick paste develops.

3. Slowly add hot milk to paste mixture while stirring vigorously.

4. If mixture isn't warm enough, heat in microwave for an additional 30 seconds.

5. Add syrup to hot mixture.

Mocha Cheesecake

8 oz. milk

1 scoop chocolate protein powder

1 tbsp. sugar-free, fat free cheesecake pudding mix

½ tsp. lemon juice OR 1 packet of True Lemon

2 tsp. instant decaffeinated espresso

3 packets no-calorie sweetener (or to taste)

> **Swap:**
>
> Don't have instant espresso? Use a good brand of instant decaf coffee instead.

To make a cold shake:

1. Combine all dry ingredients with milk in a blender.

2. For a thicker shake, blend for two minutes. For a thinner shake, blend for one minute.

3. For a thinner shake, allow liquid to settle before transferring to a glass.

4. For a thicker shake, add 5-6 cubes of ice and blend until all ice is crushed.

To make a hot drink:

1. Heat milk in microwave until hot (about 30-45 seconds).

2. Combine dry ingredients in a 12 oz. mug with 4 oz. room temperature water and stir until a thick paste develops.

3. Slowly add hot milk to paste mixture while stirring vigorously.

4. If mixture isn't warm enough, heat in microwave for an additional 30 seconds.

Banana Cheesecake

8 oz. milk

1 scoop vanilla protein powder

1 tbsp. sugar-free, fat-free cheesecake pudding mix

1 tbsp. sugar-free, fat-free banana cream cheesecake pudding mix

½ tsp. lemon juice OR 1 packet True Lemon

To make a cold shake:

1. Combine all dry ingredients with milk in a blender.

2. For a thicker shake, blend for two minutes. For a thinner shake, blend for one minute.

3. For a thinner shake, allow liquid to settle before transferring to a glass.

4. For a thicker shake, add 5-6 cubes of ice and blend until all ice is crushed.

To make a hot drink:

1. Heat milk in microwave until hot (about 30-45 seconds).

2. Combine dry ingredients in a 12 oz. mug with 4 oz. room temperature water and stir until a thick paste develops.

3. Slowly add hot milk to paste mixture while stirring vigorously.

4. If mixture isn't warm enough, heat in microwave for an additional 30 seconds.

Pumpkin Cheesecake

8 oz. milk

1 scoop vanilla protein powder

1 tbsp. sugar-free, fat-free cheesecake pudding mix

Tip:

For the hot version of this shake, try sugar-free pumpkin pie syrup instead of canned pumpkin.

3 tbsp. canned pumpkin (not pumpkin pie filling)

½ tsp. lemon juice or 1 packet True Lemon

3 packets no-calorie sweetener (or to taste)

To make a cold shake:

1. Combine all dry ingredients with milk in a blender.

2. For a thicker shake, blend for two minutes. For a thinner shake, blend for one minute.

3. For a thinner shake, allow liquid to settle before transferring to a glass.

4. For a thicker shake, add 5-6 cubes of ice and blend until all ice is crushed.

To make a hot drink:

1. Heat milk in microwave until hot (about 30-45 seconds).

2. Combine dry ingredients in a 12 oz. mug with 4 oz. room temperature water and stir until a thick paste develops.

3. Slowly add hot milk to paste mixture while stirring vigorously.

4. If mixture isn't warm enough, heat in microwave for an additional 30 seconds.

Shakes that taste like candy

W ho doesn't like candy? You? You don't? Oh…well…move past this section very quickly! But for those of you who feel like I feel…that no life is complete without at least a *little* bit of candy, read on. When you taste these shakes you won't believe they're actually good for you!

Reese's Cup

This is a slight variation from previous versions so PAY ATTENTION!

8 oz. milk

1 scoop chocolate protein powder

2 tbsp. powdered peanuts

1 packet Swiss Miss "Sensible Sweets" Diet cocoa mix

2-3 packets of no-calorie sweetener (or to taste).

To make a cold shake:

1. Combine all dry ingredients with milk in a blender.

2. For a thicker shake, blend for two minutes. For a thinner shake, blend for one minute.

3. For a thinner shake, allow liquid to settle before transferring to a glass.

4. For a thicker shake, add 5-6 cubes of ice and blend until all ice is crushed.

To make a hot drink:

1. Heat milk in microwave until hot (about 30-45 seconds).

2. Combine dry ingredients (including sweetener) in a 12 oz. mug with 4 oz. room temperature water and stir until a thick paste develops.

3. Slowly add hot milk to paste mixture while stirring vigorously.

4. If mixture isn't warm enough, heat in microwave for an additional 30 seconds.

Almond Joy

I used to love to let those suckers get all gooey and them eat them and then lick my fingers and...eh-em...what were we talking about again? Oh yeah! Shakes! Right!

8 oz. milk

1 scoop chocolate protein powder

Either 1 tbsp. German Chocolate Cake syrup or 1 tbsp. each of:

- sugar-free chocolate syrup

- sugar-free almond syrup

- sugar-free coconut syrup

2-3 packets of no-calorie sweetener (or to taste)

> Swaps:
>
> Instead of the syrups, you can use cocoa powder for the chocolate syrup along with one drop each of almond and coconut extracts.

To make a cold shake:

1. Combine all dry ingredients with milk and syrups in a blender.

2. For a thicker shake, blend for two minutes. For a thinner shake, blend for one minute.

3. For a thinner shake, allow liquid to settle before transferring to a glass.

4. For a thicker shake, add 5-6 cubes of ice and blend until all ice is crushed.

To make a hot drink:

1. Heat milk in microwave until hot (about 30-45 seconds).

2. Combine dry ingredients (including sweetener) in a 12 oz. mug with 4 oz. room temperature water and stir until a thick paste develops.

3. Slowly add hot milk to paste mixture while stirring vigorously.

4. If mixture isn't warm enough, heat in microwave for an additional 30 seconds.

5. Add syrups or extracts to hot mixture.

Peppermint Paddy

Yes there really is Peppermint Paddy syrup. I'm not making it up. Look it up and go "get the sensation!" This recipe is also different from former recipes.

8 oz. milk

1 scoop chocolate protein powder

1 packet Swiss Miss "Sensible Sweets" diet cocoa mix

2 tbsp. sugar-free peppermint paddy syrup

2 packets of no-calorie sweetener (or to taste).

To make a cold shake:

1. Combine all dry ingredients with milk and syrups in a blender.

2. For a thicker shake, blend for two minutes. For a thinner shake, blend for one minute.

3. For a thinner shake, allow liquid to settle before transferring to a glass.

4. For a thicker shake, add 5-6 cubes of ice and blend until all ice is crushed.

To make a hot drink:

1. Heat milk in microwave until hot (about 30-45 seconds).

2. Combine dry ingredients (including sweetener) in a 12 oz. mug with 4 oz. room temperature water and stir until a thick paste develops.

3. Slowly add hot milk to paste mixture while stirring vigorously.

4. If mixture isn't warm enough, heat in microwave for an additional 30 seconds.

5. Add syrup to hot mixture.

Butterfinger

Man, I love me a Butterfinger! Although I don't love that it is inextricably tied in my mind to Bart Simpson.

8 oz. milk

1 scoop chocolate protein powder

1 tbsp. sugar-free, fat-free butterscotch pudding mix

1 tbsp. powdered peanut

3 packets no-calorie sweetener (or to taste)

> **Tip:**
>
> Powdered peanut or "peanut flour" comes from grinding peanuts until most of the oil is pressed out. Search online for "peanut flour" to find it at a location near you!

To make a cold shake:

1. Combine all dry ingredients with milk in a blender.

2. For a thicker shake, blend for two minutes. For a thinner shake, blend for one minute.

3. For a thinner shake, allow liquid to settle before transferring to a glass.

4. For a thicker shake, add 5-6 cubes of ice and blend until all ice is crushed.

To make a hot drink:

1. Heat milk in microwave until hot (about 30-45 seconds).

2. Combine dry ingredients (including sweetener) in a 12 oz. mug with 4 oz. <u>room temperature</u> water and stir until a thick paste develops.

3. Slowly add hot milk to paste mixture while stirring vigorously.

4. If mixture isn't warm enough, heat in microwave for an additional 30 seconds.

Peanut Brittle

I remember getting this treat as a Christmas present as a child. As a young adult I tried to make it...an experience that ended with my favorite pan being ruined by burnt sugar and three very "not amused" firemen. Methinks this is a far safer choice post-op for many more reasons!

For that extra "oomph" try adding one drop of butter extract.

8 oz. milk

1 scoop vanilla protein powder

2 tbsp. powdered peanut

1 tbsp. sugar-free caramel syrup

To make a cold shake:

1. Combine all dry ingredients with milk in a blender.

2. For a thicker shake, blend for two minutes. For a thinner shake, blend for one minute.

3. For a thinner shake, allow liquid to settle before transferring to a glass.

4. For a thicker shake, add 5-6 cubes of ice and blend until all ice is crushed.

To make a hot drink:

1. Heat milk in microwave until hot (about 30-45 seconds).

2. Combine dry ingredients (including sweetener) in a 12 oz. mug with 4 oz. room temperature water and stir until a thick paste develops.

3. Slowly add hot milk to paste mixture while stirring vigorously.

4. If mixture isn't warm enough, heat in microwave for an additional 30 seconds.

5. Add syrup to the hot mixture.

Turtle

This wonderful confection is so wonderfully simple and gives you such a satisfaction that you won't believe you're not eating dessert! Or are you?

8 oz. milk

1 scoop chocolate protein powder

1 tbsp. sugar-free, fat-free chocolate pudding mix

1 tbsp .sugar-free Caramel syrup

> **Tip:**
>
> To take this shake to another level, top with some fat-free whipped cream and a drizzle of sugar-free caramel sauce. But just a little!

To make a cold shake:

1. Combine all dry ingredients with milk and syrup in a blender.

2. For a thicker shake, blend for two minutes. For a thinner shake, blend for one minute.

3. For a thinner shake, allow liquid to settle before transferring to a glass.

4. For a thicker shake, add 5-6 cubes of ice and blend until all ice is crushed.

To make a hot drink:

1. Heat milk in microwave until hot (about 30-45 seconds).

2. Combine dry ingredients (including sweetener) in a 12 oz. mug with 4 oz. <u>room temperature</u> water and stir until a thick paste develops.

3. Slowly add hot milk to paste mixture while stirring vigorously.

4. If mixture isn't warm enough, heat in microwave for an additional 30 seconds.

5. Add syrup to the hot mixture.

Coffeehouse & Restaurant Knock-Offs

Were you addicted to your favorite coffeehouse drink? These trade-offs will give you the same satisfaction while sparing both your waistline *and* your wallet. And, as an added bonus, you can call yourself a barista!

Basic Protein Coffee

8 oz. boiling water

2 tsp. instant decaffeinated coffee

4 oz. room temperature water

1 scoop protein powder

No-Calorie sweetener, to taste

Optional: non-dairy or other creamer to taste.

To make a cold coffee shake:

1. Combine all dry ingredients with milk in a blender (omit water and creamer).

2. For a thicker shake, blend for two minutes. For a thinner shake, blend for one minute.

3. For a thinner shake, allow liquid to settle before transferring to a glass.

4. For a thicker shake, add 5-6 cubes of ice and blend until all ice is crushed.

To make a hot coffee drink:

1. Combine protein powder, coffee, sweetener and any syrups in a 12 oz. mug with room temperature water and stir until thick paste develops.

2. Slowly add boiling water while stirring paste vigorously.

3. Add creamer or any other flavorings as desired.

Basic Protein "Fake" Latte

Notice I didn't give a protein powder flavor? If you like a mocha, use chocolate. Or use vanilla or even unflavored protein to just have your coffee taste.

8 oz. heated milk

4 oz. room temperature water

1 scoop protein powder

2 tsp instant decaffeinated espresso powder

No-calorie sweetener, to taste

Optional: non-dairy or other creamer to taste.

To make an iced latte:

1. Follow the directions for making a hot latte.

2. Add to a larger glass of ice.

To make a hot latte:

1. Combine protein powder, coffee, sweetener and any syrups in a 12 oz. mug with room temperature water and stir until thick paste develops.

2. Heat milk in a microwave until hot.

3. Slowly add hot milk while stirring paste vigorously.

4. Add creamer or any other flavorings as desired.

Decaf Mochaccino Frapp

While the term "Frapp" implies a cold drink, I give instructions on how to make it hot if that's how you prefer.

8 oz. milk

1 scoop chocolate protein powder

2 tsp decaffeinated instant espresso

1 tbsp unsweetened cocoa powder

1 tbsp no-calorie sweetener

1 tbsp of your favorite sugar-free syrup (caramel and hazelnut are good to start)

To make a cold shake:

1. Combine all dry ingredients with milk and syrup in a blender

2. For a thicker shake, blend for two minutes. For a thinner shake, blend for one minute.

3. For a thinner shake, allow liquid to settle before transferring to a glass.

4. For a thicker shake, add 5-6 cubes of ice and blend until all ice is crushed.

To make a hot drink:

1. Heat milk in microwave until hot (about 30-45 seconds)

2. Combine dry ingredients (including sweetener) in a 12 oz. mug with 4 oz. room temperature water and stir until a thick paste develops.

3. Slowly add hot milk to paste mixture while stirring vigorously.

4. If mixture isn't warm enough, heat in microwave for an additional 30 seconds.

5. Add syrup to hot mixture.

Vanilla Frapp

8 oz. milk

2 tsp. instant decaffeinated espresso powder

1 tbsp. sugar-free, fat-free vanilla pudding mix

1 scoop vanilla protein powder

1 tbsp. no-calorie sweetener

> **Swap:**
>
> Don't have instant espresso? Use a good brand of instant decaffeinated coffee instead.

To make a cold shake:

1. Combine all dry ingredients with milk in a blender.

2. For a thicker shake, blend for two minutes. For a thinner shake, blend for one minute.

3. For a thinner shake, allow liquid to settle before transferring to a glass.

4. For a thicker shake, add 5-6 cubes of ice and blend until all ice is crushed.

To make a hot drink:

1. Heat milk in microwave until hot (about 30-45 seconds).

2. Combine dry ingredients in a 12 oz. mug with 4 oz. room temperature water and stir until a thick paste develops.

3. Slowly add hot milk to paste mixture while stirring vigorously.

4. If mixture isn't warm enough, heat in microwave for an additional 30 seconds.

Banana Mocha Frapp

This is one of those shakes I didn't think I'd like until I actually tried it. Now I love it!

8 oz. milk

1 scoop chocolate protein powder

2 tsp. instant decaffeinated espresso powder

2 packets of no-calorie sweetener

½ frozen banana

> **Tip:**
>
> For a bit more decadence, mix 2 tbsp sugar-free caramel syrup (like Smucker's) with 2 tbsp fat-free whipped cream to top your shake.

To make a cold shake:

1. Combine all dry ingredients with milk in a blender.

2. For a thicker shake, blend for two minutes. For a thinner shake, blend for one minute.

3. For a thinner shake, add banana, blend again and then allow liquid to settle before transferring to a glass.

4. For a thicker shake, add banana and 5-6 ice cubes and blend until are crushed.

To make a hot drink:

1. Heat milk in microwave until hot (about 30-45 seconds).

2. Combine dry ingredients (including sweetener) in a 12 oz. mug with 4 oz. room temperature water and stir until a thick paste develops.

3. Slowly add hot milk to paste mixture while stirring vigorously.

4. If mixture isn't warm enough, heat in microwave for an additional 30 seconds.

Mint Mocha Frapp

This tastes like a Thin Mint cookie for grown-ups!

8 oz. milk

1 scoop chocolate protein powder

2 tsp. instant decaffeinated espresso powder

2 packets of no-calorie sweetener

2 tbsp. sugar-free Peppermint Paddy syrup

To make a cold shake:

1. Combine all dry ingredients with milk and syrup in a blender

2. For a thicker shake, blend for two minutes. For a thinner shake, blend for one minute.

3. For a thinner shake, allow liquid to settle before transferring to a glass.

4. For a thicker shake, add 5-6 cubes of ice and blend until all ice is crushed.

To make a hot drink:

1. Heat milk in microwave until hot (about 30-45 seconds)

2. Combine dry ingredients (including sweetener) in a 12 oz. mug with 4 oz. room temperature water and stir until a thick paste develops.

3. Slowly add hot milk to paste mixture while stirring vigorously.

4. If mixture isn't warm enough, heat in microwave for an additional 30 seconds.

5. Add syrup to hot mixture.

Peanut Butter Mocha

8 oz. milk

1 scoop chocolate protein powder

2 tsp. instant decaffeinated espresso powder

2 tbsp. powdered peanut

2 packets of no-calorie sweetener

To make a cold shake:

1. Combine all dry ingredients with milk in a blender

2. For a thicker shake, blend for two minutes. For a thinner shake, blend for one minute.

3. For a thinner shake, allow liquid to settle before transferring to a glass.

4. For a thicker shake, add 5-6 cubes of ice and blend until all ice is crushed.

To make a hot drink:

1. Heat milk in microwave until hot (about 30-45 seconds)

2. Combine dry ingredients (including sweetener) in a 12 oz. mug with 4 oz. room temperature water and stir until a thick paste develops.

3. Slowly add hot milk to paste mixture while stirring vigorously.

4. If mixture isn't warm enough, heat in microwave for an additional 30 seconds.

Coffee Toffee Balanced Frosty

When Wendy's came out with their Coffee-Toffee drink I knew I'd have to make a protein variation. This one keeps the great flavor of the drink while giving you mega-protein!

8 oz. milk

1 scoop vanilla protein powder

1 tsp. instant decaffeinated coffee

2 tbsp. sugar-free English toffee syrup

1 tbsp. sugar-free, fat-free butterscotch pudding mix

To make a cold shake:

1. Combine all dry ingredients with milk and syrup in a blender.

2. For a thicker shake, blend for two minutes. For a thinner shake, blend for one minute.

3. For a thinner shake, allow liquid to settle before transferring to a glass.

4. For a thicker shake, add 5-6 cubes of ice and blend until all ice is crushed.

To make a hot drink:

1. Heat milk in microwave until hot (about 30-45 seconds).

2. Combine dry ingredients (including sweetener) in a 12 oz. mug with 4 oz. room temperature water and stir until a thick paste develops.

3. Slowly add hot milk to paste mixture while stirring vigorously.

4. If mixture isn't warm enough, heat in microwave for an additional 30 seconds.

5. Add syrup to hot mixture.

Banana smoothie

Since these next few are smoothie recipes, I give only the cold preparation directions. Take this smoothie to the next level with frozen berries, a great source of fiber and anti-oxidants!

8 oz. milk or unflavored yogurt

1 scoop vanilla protein powder

½ - 1 whole frozen banana

2 tbsp. sugar-free vanilla syrup

To make a cold shake:

1. Combine all dry ingredients with milk and syrup in a blender.

2. For a thicker shake, blend for two minutes. For a thinner shake, blend for one minute.

3. For a thinner shake, allow liquid to settle before transferring to a glass.

4. For a thicker shake, add 5-6 cubes of ice and blend until all ice is crushed.

Green Tea Smoothie

8 oz. milk

1 scoop vanilla protein powder

1-2 tsp. green tea powder (or 4 oz. brewed green tea)

1 tbsp. sugar-free, fat-free vanilla pudding

2 packets no-calorie sweetener

Swap:

In the absence of green tea powder, you can use 6 oz. milk + a concentrated green tea (2 oz. water + green tea bag. Allow to steep 3 minutes, remove and use).

To make a cold shake:

1. Combine all dry ingredients with milk in a blender.

2. For a thicker shake, blend for two minutes. For a thinner shake, blend for one minute.

3. For a thinner shake, allow liquid to settle before transferring to a glass.

4. For a thicker shake, add 5-6 cubes of ice and blend until all ice is crushed.

Iced Tea

Have you ever had this? If so you know it is soooo yummy! For special occasions, I would say one could probably justify using light coconut milk instead of cow's milk. For everyday use, follow the recipe below for fewer calories.

4 oz. milk

4 oz. cold water

1 sugar-free iced tea drink stick

1 scoop vanilla protein powder

2 tbsp. sugar-free coconut syrup

3-4 packets of no-calorie sweetener (or to taste)

To make a cold shake:

1. Combine all dry ingredients with milk and syrup in a blender.

2. For a thicker shake, blend for two minutes. For a thinner shake, blend for one minute.

3. For a thinner shake, allow liquid to settle before transferring to a glass.

4. For a thicker shake, add 5-6 cubes of ice and blend until all ice is crushed.

Chai Latte

This Indian drink is becoming ever popular in American coffeehouses. Make this simple recipe to bring the flavors of chai to your protein shake!

8 oz. milk
1 scoop vanilla protein powder
1 tbsp. butterscotch pudding mix
2 tbsp. sugar-free chai concentrate

> Swap:
> Chai Concentrate can be hard to find. If you can't find it, there are many sugar-free chai mixes available in stores. Pick the one with the least amount of calories and carbohydrates and use only one portion!

To make a cold shake:

1. Combine all dry ingredients with milk in a blender.

2. For a thicker shake, blend for two minutes. For a thinner shake, blend for one minute.

3. For a thinner shake, allow liquid to settle before transferring to a glass.

4. For a thicker shake, add 5-6 cubes of ice and blend until all ice is crushed.

To make a hot drink:

1. Heat milk in microwave until hot (about 30-45 seconds).

2. Combine dry ingredients (including sweetener) in a 12 oz. mug with 4 oz. room temperature water and stir until a thick paste develops.

3. Slowly add hot milk to paste mixture while stirring vigorously.

4. If mixture isn't warm enough, heat in microwave for an additional 30 seconds.

Irish Coffee

You won't even miss the whiskey in this spin on the classic Irish drink!

8 oz. milk
1 scoop vanilla protein powder
1 tsp. instant decaffeinated coffee
3 or 4 pumps sugar-free Irish Cream syrup

To make a cold shake:

1. Combine all dry ingredients with milk and syrup in a blender.

2. For a thicker shake, blend for two minutes. For a thinner shake, blend for one minute.

3. For a thinner shake, allow liquid to settle before transferring to a glass.

4. For a thicker shake, add 5-6 cubes of ice and blend until all ice is crushed.

To make a hot drink:

1. Heat milk in microwave until hot (about 30-45 seconds).

2. Combine dry ingredients (including sweetener) in a 12 oz. mug with 4 oz. room temperature water and stir until a thick paste develops.

3. Slowly add hot milk to paste mixture while stirring vigorously.

4. If mixture isn't warm enough, heat in microwave for an additional 30 seconds.

5. Add syrup to the hot mixture.

Mudslide

Have any of you ever tried a Mudslide? They sell them in restaurants. They are about a million calories but you sip it and feel like you could die right then and there a happy individual. I much prefer this as a cold shake or as ice cream...but your mileage may vary!

8 oz. milk (use regular skim or 2%)

1 scoop cookies 'n cream protein powder

1 tbsp. sugar-free Kahlua flavored syrup,

1 pkg. Swiss Miss "Sensible Sweets" diet cocoa mix

2-3 packets of no-calorie sweetener (to taste).

To make a cold shake:

1. Combine all dry ingredients with milk in a blender.

2. For a thicker shake, blend for two minutes. For a thinner shake, blend for one minute.

3. For a thinner shake, allow liquid to settle before transferring to a glass.

4. For a thicker shake, add 5-6 cubes of ice and blend until all ice is crushed.

To make a hot drink:

1. Heat milk in microwave until hot (about 30-45 seconds).

2. Combine dry ingredients (including sweetener) in a 12 oz. mug with 4 oz. room temperature water and stir until a thick paste develops.

3. Slowly add hot milk to paste mixture while stirring vigorously.

4. If mixture isn't warm enough, heat in microwave for an additional 30 seconds.

5. Add syrup to the hot mixture.

60

Standard Frozen Hot Chocolate

Ever since Paula Deen introduced me to this drink (after surgery...gee thanks!) I have wanted one. Here's my interpretation.

8 oz. milk

1 scoop chocolate protein powder

1 packet Swiss Miss "Sensible Sweets" diet cocoa mix

1 tbsp. sugar-free chocolate syrup (not the no-calorie kind...like Hershey's)

2-3 packets of no-calorie sweetener (or to taste)

Tip:

Use 1 or 2% milk for a richer flavor

To make a cold shake:

1. Combine all dry ingredients with milk and syrup in a blender.

2. For a thicker shake, blend for two minutes. For a thinner shake, blend for one minute.

3. For a thinner shake, allow liquid to settle before transferring to a glass.

4. For a thicker shake, add 5-6 cubes of ice and blend until all ice is crushed.

Kahlua and Scream!

For those who love the taste of Kahlua WITHOUT the chocolate.

8 oz. milk

1 scoop vanilla protein powder

1 tbsp. sugar-free, fat-free vanilla pudding mix

2 tbsp. sugar-free Kahlua flavored syrup

Ice

To make a cold shake:

1. Combine all dry ingredients with milk in a blender.

2. For a thicker shake, blend for two minutes. For a thinner shake, blend for one minute.

3. For a thinner shake, allow liquid to settle before transferring to a glass.

4. For a thicker shake, add 5-6 cubes of ice and blend until all ice is crushed.

To make a hot drink:

1. Heat milk in microwave until hot (about 30-45 seconds).

2. Combine dry ingredients in a 12 oz. mug with 4 oz. room temperature water and stir until a thick paste develops.

3. Slowly add hot milk to paste mixture while stirring vigorously.

4. If mixture isn't warm enough, heat in microwave for an additional 30 seconds.

Seasonal Protein Shakes

There are certain flavors we'll always associate with certain times of the year—pumpkin and cinnamon with fall, nutmeg and egg nog at Christmastime, fresh fruity flavors in the summer. These shakes celebrate the seasons while honoring your commitment to a new lifestyle.

Apple Cider

6 oz. water

1 packet sugar-free apple cider mix (there is one by the name of Alpine that is very nice)

1 scoop of unflavored protein powder

2-3 packets of no-calorie sweetener (or to taste)

To make a cold shake:

1. Combine all ingredients in a blender.

2. Blend for 1 minute then add 5-6 ice cubes and blend again until all ice is crushed.

To make a hot drink:

1. Boil or heat 8 oz. water.

2. Combine protein powder, cider mix, sweetener and 4 oz. room temperature water and stir until a thick paste develops.

3. Slowly add hot water to paste mixture while stirring vigorously.

4. If mixture isn't warm enough, heat in microwave for an additional 30 seconds.

Pumpkin Spice

This one requires a special order (the cappuccino mix), but it is sooooo worth it. This is the ONLY shake you'll see on this whole recipe list that doesn't require additional sweetening.

8 oz. milk

1 scoop vanilla protein powder

2 scoops Ron & Frank's Skinny Gourmet pumpkin spice cappuccino mix (25 calories for 2 scoops!)

OR

1 tbsp. canned pumpkin (not pumpkin pie filling) + 1/8 tsp. pumpkin pie spice

To make a cold shake:	To make a hot drink:
1. Combine all dry ingredients with milk in a blender.	1. Heat milk in microwave until hot (about 30-45 seconds).
2. For a thicker shake, blend for two minutes. For a thinner shake, blend for one minute.	2. Combine dry ingredients in a 12 oz. mug with 4 oz. room temperature water and stir until a thick paste develops.
3. For a thinner shake, allow liquid to settle before transferring to a glass.	3. Slowly add hot milk to paste mixture while stirring vigorously.
4. For a thicker shake, add 5-6 cubes of ice and blend until all ice is crushed.	4. If mixture isn't warm enough, heat in microwave for an additional 30 seconds.

Egg Nog

This is a nice alternative to the real thing which would send me on a Christmas vacation to "dumps-ville."

Milk

1 scoop vanilla protein powder

2 tbsp. sugar-free egg nog syrup

1 tbsp. sugar-free, fat free vanilla pudding mix

2-3 packets of no-calorie sweetener (or to taste)

Tip:

In absence of egg nog flavored syrup you can use 1 drop rum extract + 1 tbsp. pumpkin pie spice and it gives a good proximity.

To make a cold shake:

1. Combine all dry ingredients with milk and syrup in a blender.

2. For a thicker shake, blend for two minutes. For a thinner shake, blend for one minute.

3. For a thinner shake, allow liquid to settle before transferring to a glass.

4. For a thicker shake, add 5-6 cubes of ice and blend until all ice is crushed.

Candy Cane

I hang dozens of candy canes on my Christmas tree every year. And I suppose I could go for the sugar-free variety, but I am a purist. But now I don't have to miss the taste of my beloved Christmas goody.

4 oz. water

1 scoop vanilla protein powder

3 tbsp. sugar-free peppermint syrup

2-3 packets no-calorie sweetener (or to taste)

> **Tip:**
>
> In the absence of peppermint syrup, you can use 1/8 tsp. of peppermint extract. Be careful with extracts. A little goes a LONG way!

To make a cold shake:

1. Combine all dry ingredients with milk and syrup in a blender.

2. For a thicker shake, blend for two minutes. For a thinner shake, blend for one minute.

3. For a thinner shake, allow liquid to settle before transferring to a glass.

4. For a thicker shake, add 5-6 cubes of ice and blend until all ice is crushed.

To make a hot drink:

1. Heat milk in microwave until hot (about 30-45 seconds).

2. Combine dry ingredients (including sweetener) in a 12 oz. mug with 4 oz. room temperature water and stir until a thick paste develops.

3. Slowly add hot milk to paste mixture while stirring vigorously.

4. If mixture isn't warm enough, heat in microwave for an additional 30 seconds.

5. Add syrup or extract to hot mixture.

Gingerbread

The comforting smell of this shake is enough to make it feel like Christmas!

8 oz. milk

1 scoop vanilla protein powder

2 tbsp. sugar-free gingerbread syrup

1 tbsp. sugar-free, fat-free butterscotch pudding mix

2-3 packets no-calorie sweetener (or to taste)

> Swap:
>
> If you don't have sugar-free gingerbread syrup you could use a pinch of ground ginger + a pinch of pumpkin pie spice.

To make a cold shake:

1. Combine all dry ingredients with milk and syrup in a blender.

2. For a thicker shake, blend for two minutes. For a thinner shake, blend for one minute.

3. For a thinner shake, allow liquid to settle before transferring to a glass.

4. For a thicker shake, add 5-6 cubes of ice and blend until all ice is crushed.

To make a hot drink:

1. Heat milk in microwave until hot (about 30-45 seconds).

2. Combine dry ingredients (including sweetener) in a 12 oz. mug with 4 oz. room temperature water and stir until a thick paste develops.

3. Slowly add hot milk to paste mixture while stirring vigorously.

4. If mixture isn't warm enough, heat in microwave for an additional 30 seconds.

"Peeps" Shake

Ok, so this is more of a marshmallow shake but I do it up to look like a peeps shake. Here's how I do it:

8 oz. milk

1 scoop vanilla protein powder

2 tbsp. sugar-free marshmallow syrup

2-3 packets no-calorie sweetener (or to taste)

1-2 drops yellow food coloring

> **Tip:**
>
> If you want to go that extra mile, serve it with some fat-free whipped cream and a LIGHT dusting of Splenda that has been tinted a nice contrasting color...like PINK!

To make a cold shake:

1. Combine all dry ingredients with milk and syrup in a blender.

2. For a thicker shake, blend for two minutes. For a thinner shake, blend for one minute.

3. For a thinner shake, allow liquid to settle before transferring to a glass.

4. For a thicker shake, add 5-6 cubes of ice and blend until all ice is crushed.

To make a hot drink:

1. Heat milk in microwave until hot (about 30-45 seconds).

2. Combine dry ingredients (including sweetener, omit extract) in a 12 oz. mug with 4 oz. room temperature water and stir until a thick paste develops.

3. Slowly add hot milk to paste mixture while stirring vigorously.

4. If mixture isn't warm enough, heat in microwave for an additional 30 seconds.

5. Add syrup to hot mixture.

Fruity Protein Drinks

Not everyone is a "milky drink" drinker. For those of you who love yourself a good fruit smoothie…this section is for YOU!

The Raven

I call this the Raven because I am from Baltimore and in Baltimore during the football season, you see LOTS of purple. So I had to give love to the home team!

4 oz. water

4 oz. unflavored, fat-free Greek yogurt

1 cup fresh blueberries

1 scoop Nectar Twisted Cherry protein powder

1 packet of "True Lemon" (or a tsp of fresh lemon juice)

5 –6 ice cubes

Directions:

1. Combine all ingredients except ice in a blender.

2. Blend for 1 minute or until frozen fruit is completely pulverized.

3. Add ice and blend again until all ice is crushed.

Strawberry-Banana Smoothie

4 oz. water

4 oz. unflavored, fat-free Greek yogurt

½ a frozen banana

1 c. frozen strawberries

1 scoop strawberry protein powder

5-6 ice cubes

Directions:

1. Combine all ingredients except ice in a blender.

2. Blend for 1 minute or until frozen fruit is completely pulverized.

3. Add ice and blend again until all ice is crushed.

Protein Piña Colada

4 oz. water

½ frozen banana

½ c. frozen pineapple cubes (make sure they were packed in water not in syrup of ANY kind)

1 c. fresh strawberries

Tip:

Want this drink but can't afford the carbs? Invest in a box of Baja Bob's sugar-free Pina Colada mix! Details on where to buy in the Resources section.

1 tbsp sugar-free Toasted Coconut Syrup, 6-8 ice cubes

No-calorie sweetener, to taste

Directions:

1. Combine all dry ingredients with milk in a blender.

2. For a thicker shake, blend for two minutes. For a thinner shake, blend for one minute.

3. For a thinner shake, allow liquid to settle before transferring to a glass.

4. For a thicker shake, add 5-6 cubes of ice and blend until all ice is crushed.

Lemon Sorbet

8 oz. water

1 stick sugar free lemonade drink mix

1 scoop Nectar Roadside Lemonade protein powder

6-8 ice cubes

Tip:

Double any of the sorbet recipes to make a sorbet base to use in your ice cream maker!

Directions:

1. Combine all dry ingredients with milk in a blender.

2. For a thicker shake, blend for two minutes. For a thinner shake, blend for one minute.

3. For a thinner shake, allow liquid to settle before transferring to a glass.

4. For a thicker shake, add 5-6 cubes of ice and blend until all ice is crushed.

Raspberry Sorbet

6 oz. water

1 scoop unflavored protein powder

1 c. frozen raspberries

1 tbsp. sugar-free raspberry syrup

1 packet True Lemon

No-calorie sweetener, to taste

5-6 ice cubes

Directions:

1. Combine everything except ice in a blender.

2. Blend 1 minute or until all the berries are pulverized.

3. Add ice and blend again until all ice is crushed.

Some "Out of the Box" Shakes

This simply means I couldn't fit them into a particular category. Some are a little whacky, but I promise you that I have tried each and every shake recipe in this section (and in this book). If you're ever in the mood for something different, give one of these shakes a try. You never know, you just mike like them!

White chocolate hazelnut

8 oz. milk

1 scoop vanilla protein powder

1 tbsp. sugar-free, fat-free white chocolate pudding mix

1 tbsp. sugar free hazelnut syrup

2-4 packets of no-calorie sweetener (to taste)

To make a cold shake:

1. Combine all dry ingredients with milk and syrup in a blender.

2. For a thicker shake, blend for two minutes. For a thinner shake, blend for one minute.

3. For a thinner shake, allow liquid to settle before transferring to a glass.

4. For a thicker shake, add 5-6 cubes of ice and blend until all ice is crushed.

To make a hot drink:

1. Heat milk in microwave until hot (about 30-45 seconds).

2. Combine dry ingredients (including sweetener) in a 12 oz. mug with 4 oz. room temperature water and stir until a thick paste develops.

3. Slowly add hot milk to paste mixture while stirring vigorously.

4. If mixture isn't warm enough, heat in microwave for an additional 30 seconds.

5. Add syrup to hot mixture

Cinnamon Cream Tea

4 oz. milk

4 oz. prepared tea of your choice

1 scoop vanilla protein powder

1 tbsp. sugar-free hazelnut syrup

1 tsp. cinnamon

Tip:

Make this recipe with a cinnamon flavored herbal tea—it will intensify the cinnamon flavor and herbal tea is decaffeinated so it counts toward your

To make a cold shake:

1. Combine all dry ingredients with milk and syrup in a blender.

2. For a thicker shake, blend for two minutes. For a thinner shake, blend for one minute.

3. For a thinner shake, allow liquid to settle before transferring to a glass.

4. For a thicker shake, add 5-6 cubes of ice and blend until all ice is crushed.

To make a hot drink:

1. Heat milk in microwave until hot (about 30-45 seconds).

2. Combine dry ingredients (including sweetener) in a 12 oz. mug with 4 oz. room temperature water and stir until a thick paste develops.

3. Slowly add hot milk to paste mixture while stirring vigorously.

4. If mixture isn't warm enough, heat in microwave for an additional 30 seconds.

5. Add syrup to hot mixture.

Orange Creamsicle

8 oz. milk

1 scoop vanilla protein powder

1 packet orange flavored sugar-free drink stick

(the kind you put in a water bottle)

1 tbsp sugar-free, fat-free vanilla pudding mix

1 tbsp sugar-free vanilla syrup

Directions:

1. Combine all dry ingredients with milk in a blender.

2. For a thicker shake, blend for two minutes. For a thinner shake, blend for one minute.

3. For a thinner shake, allow liquid to settle before transferring to a glass.

4. For a thicker shake, add 5-6 cubes of ice and blend until all ice is crushed.

Lemon meringue pie

8 oz. milk

1 scoop vanilla protein powder

1 stick sugar-free lemonade mix

1 tbsp. sugar-free, fat-free lemon pudding mix

1 tbsp. sugar-free vanilla syrup

Directions:

1. Combine all dry ingredients with milk in a blender.

2. For a thicker shake, blend for two minutes. For a thinner shake, blend for one minute.

3. For a thinner shake, allow liquid to settle before transferring to a glass.

4. For a thicker shake, add 5-6 cubes of ice and blend until all ice is crushed.

Neopolitan

Remember when you were a kid and used to LOVE to eat Neopolitan ice cream (for me that would preferably be in the form of "ice cream soup")? This shake captures those tastes perfectly, transporting you straight back to your childhood!

8 oz. milk

1 scoop vanilla protein powder

1 cup frozen strawberries

1 tbsp. unsweetened cocoa powder

3-5 packets no-calorie sweetener

Ice

Directions:

1. Combine all dry ingredients with milk in a blender.

2. For a thicker shake, blend for two minutes. For a thinner shake, blend for one minute.

3. For a thinner shake, allow liquid to settle before transferring to a glass.

4. For a thicker shake, add 5-6 cubes of ice and blend until all ice is crushed.

Peanut Butter & Jelly

It's peanut butter jelly time! Peanut butter jelly time!

8 oz. milk

1 scoop vanilla protein powder

2 tbsp powdered peanut

2 tbsp sugar-free raspberry syrup

No-calorie sweetener, to taste

> **Tip:**
>
> Powdered peanut is sold online as "PB2."

Directions:

1. Combine all dry ingredients with milk and syrup in a blender

2. For a thicker shake, blend for two minutes. For a thinner shake, blend for one minute.

3. For a thinner shake, allow liquid to settle before transferring to a glass.

4. For a thicker shake, add 5-6 cubes of ice and blend until all ice is crushed.

Coconut Curry

Don't scratch your head…it really is good! Curries can be savory or they can be sweet. This one is what I call a "grown folk" drink. It is smooth and sophisticated and will make you wonder if you are really drinking what you think you're drinking.

8 oz. milk

1 scoop vanilla protein powder

¼ tsp curry powder

2 tbsp sugar-free toasted coconut syrup

a dash of cinnamon

No-calorie sweetener, to taste

To make a cold shake:

1. Combine all dry ingredients with milk and syrup in a blender

2. For a thicker shake, blend for two minutes. For a thinner shake, blend for one minute.

3. For a thinner shake, allow liquid to settle before transferring to a glass.

4. For a thicker shake, add 5-6 cubes of ice and blend until all ice is crushed.

To make a hot drink:

1. Heat milk in microwave until hot (about 30-45 seconds)

2. Combine dry ingredients (including sweetener) in a 12 oz. mug with 4 oz. room temperature water and stir until a thick paste develops.

3. Slowly add hot milk to paste mixture while stirring vigorously.

4. If mixture isn't warm enough, heat in microwave for an additional 30 seconds.

5. Add syrup to hot mixture.

Mexican Hot Chocolate

I sometimes contemplate if the Mexicans were really the first ones to think of putting cocoa and cinnamon together or if they just got credit for a good thing. No matter…it's still good!

8 oz. milk

1 scoop chocolate protein powder

1 packet Swiss Miss "Sensible Sweets" diet cocoa mix

1-2 tbsp. sugar-free cinnamon syrup

2-3 packets no-calorie sweetener (or to taste)

To make a cold shake:

1. Combine all dry ingredients with milk in a blender.

2. For a thicker shake, blend for two minutes. For a thinner shake, blend for one minute.

3. For a thinner shake, allow liquid to settle before transferring to a glass.

4. For a thicker shake, add 5-6 cubes of ice and blend until all ice is crushed.

To make a hot drink:

1. Heat milk in microwave until hot (about 30-45 seconds).

2. Combine dry ingredients in a 12 oz. mug with 4 oz. room temperature water and stir until a thick paste develops.

3. Slowly add hot milk to paste mixture while stirring vigorously.

4. If mixture isn't warm enough, heat in microwave for an additional 30 seconds.

Chocolate Orange Liquer Protein Shake

8 oz. milk
1 scoop chocolate protein powder
1 tbsp. unsweetened cocoa powder
1 tbsp. sugar-free butter rum syrup
2 packets True Orange
1 tablespoon no-calorie sweetener

> Swap:
>
> If you don't want to invest in a whole bottle of sugar-free Butter Rum syrup, <u>one drop</u> of rum extract works just fine. And, no, there is no alcohol in rum ex-

To make a cold shake:

1. Combine all dry ingredients with milk in a blender.

2. For a thicker shake, blend for two minutes. For a thinner shake, blend for one minute.

3. For a thinner shake, allow liquid to settle before transferring to a glass.

4. For a thicker shake, add 5-6 cubes of ice and blend until all ice is crushed.

To make a hot drink:

1. Heat milk in microwave until hot (about 30-45 seconds).

2. Combine dry ingredients in a 12 oz. mug with 4 oz. <u>room temperature</u> water and stir until a thick paste develops.

3. Slowly add hot milk to paste mixture while stirring vigorously.

4. If mixture isn't warm enough, heat in microwave for an additional 30 seconds.

Your Protein Test Kitchen

You've read my recipes and methods – now it's your turn! Use this worksheet to invent your own protein shake recipes. If you come up with anything good, e-mail it to me at bariatricfoodie@yahoo.com so I can feature it on the blog!

Type of Shake:

Cold Shake   Hot Drink   Frozen Treat

If a frozen treat:

Ice Cream   Gelato   Sorbet

Blizzard   Popsicle

Test Recipe

Ingredient	Amount	Stats (Calories, Protein, Carbs, etc.) for ingredient
Total shake stats:		

Did you like this recipe? Yes   No

If no, what didn't you like about it?

How will you change it to make it better?

Ingredient	Amount	Stats (Calories, Protein, Carbs, etc.
Total shake stats:		

Bariatric Foodie Guide to Measurements and Conversions

Your Final Recipe:

This	=	This
3 tsp	=	1 tbsp
2 tbsp	=	1 oz.
2 oz.	=	¼ cup
4 oz.	=	½ cup
8 oz.	=	1 cup
16 oz.	=	1 lb.
1 tbsp sugar free syrup	=	1 pump

Troubleshooting Your Shake

It happens to the best of us. You do everything right and yet your shake is so...wrong! Here are some common problems and solutions to make your next shake better.

Help My Shake is...	Possible Problem	How to Fix it
My (non-Triple X) shake is too frothy/foamy!	Froth and foam develop when air mixes into your shake.	Unfortunately, air is unavoidable. However, it can help to let your shake "settle" in the blender for a minute or two before pouring it into your glass. Also, after you pour it, use a spoon to gently stir the foam *into* the shake. It won't get rid of all the foam, but it does help!
I tried the Triple X method and it didn't work! My shake is not thick!	The problem is usually one of two things: Using water as the base of your protein shake the size of your blender. Larger blenders tend to present more of a challenge than smaller ones.	Always use milk as the base for a Triple X shake. If you have a larger blender, use less liquid and more ice. If that doesn't help, consider either adding additional dry milk (to a reduced amount of liquid) or using a half yogurt/half milk base.
My shake is too sweet!	Look at what you added to it. Often when we add things like pudding mix or fruit, no additional sweetener is needed, especially when you use very ripe fresh fruit.	If you have some in your refrigerator, add two heaping tablespoons of cottage cheese to your shake mix and re-blend. Trust me, you won't be able to tell it's in there. Cottage cheese is bland and slightly bitter, so it will counter the sweetness and calm the flavor down.

My shake isn't sweet enough.	Remember, making cold drinks dulls the sweetness.	Besides the obvious – adding more sweetener – taste test your shake as you add more to make sure you don't add too much!
My shake is bitter!	I hear this a lot from people who have incorporated baking cocoa into their protein shake recipes (several of my recipes call for it). Other possible culprits are using cottage cheese as a shake base (none of my recipes call for it but some people do it since cottage cheese has about the same calories as a cup of milk but about 6 more grams of protein).	If the culprit is cocoa powder, remember you need to offset the bitterness with sweetness. Add a little extra no-calorie sweetener and that SHOULD solve the problem. If you've used cottage cheese as your shake base, add a bit of lemon juice to your shake, along with a little extra sweetener. That should even the flavor out!
My chocolate shake doesn't taste chocolatey.	This is usually the result of ignoring one of the most basic pieces of advice I give about chocolate recipes. See the solution to find out what it is…	When I say put a teaspoon of instant coffee in your chocolate shake, it isn't because I'm trying to make you a coffee convert! A small bit of coffee plays up the flavor of chocolate. You won't taste the coffee, you WILL taste the intense chocolate flavor!
The shake I loved before my surgery tastes yucky now!	Unfortunately, this probably doesn't have anything to do with the ingredients in your shake. Bariatric surgery, especially gastric bypass, can affect your sweetness tolerance and after surgery *everything* can taste too sweet.	Gradually your sweetness threshold will become more normal. Until then, try not adding any additional sweetener to your protein shake. If it's still too sweet, ditch the sugar-free syrup too and try to find something that mimics the taste without the added sweetener (ground cinnamon vs. cinnamon flavored syrup).

I can smell the protein no matter what I do to my shake…and I hate it! What do I do?	Protein powder is always going to be protein powder. We can manipulate it and add things to it, but it is what it is.	If the smell of the shake prohibits you from drinking it, my first suggestion is to investigate other protein powders. Again, the "right" shake for you is the one you can stand ingesting! If buying a new protein powder isn't an option right now, I'd suggest investing in a sports bottle. If the flavor of your shake is fine but the smell is off, a sports bottle lid will keep you from smelling your shake as you drink it.
My shake makes me queasy!	This could be for several reasons. It may be that: You can no longer tolerate lactose (milk sugar). It doesn't matter if you were not lactose intolerant before surgery, you can become so after. You may not be able to tolerate whey protein. The additives in your shake may have produced too many carbs or sugar alcohols for your system to handle.	The solution depends largely on the reason: If you determine that you are lactose intolerant, you can try using whey isolate. That should resolve your problem. If you are whey intolerant, you should investigate soy or other kinds of protein supplements. To determine if your shake additives are making you sick, simply try making a shake without them and doing a "sip test" (taking a sip and waiting a few minutes for a reaction). If you don't get sick from it, try adding back ingredients, one at a time, to see how much you can handle. None of the shake recipes in this book have a great amount of sugar alcohols or carbs but every system is different!

Resources

Throughout this book you'll see that I've listed a lot of specialty items that you might consider buying to enhance your protein shakes. In most cases throughout the book, where there is a specialty item, I've also recommended a product you can find in your local store. Whether or not to invest in any of the products I've listed is up to you. You can certainly have great shakes with or without them!

For those interested in investing in some of the products I've listed, here's where to get them.

Sugar-free syrups

The sugar-free syrups I list in my protein shake recipes are no-calorie, no sugar, no carbohydrate syrups that are commonly used in coffee shops to make sugar-free coffee drinks. The three most common brands are Torani, DaVinci and Starbucks.

Torani/DaVinci Syrups

There are places, both online and locally, that you can go to get these syrups. Online, the best value I've found is at **Netrition (www.netrition.com)**. The syrups are reasonably priced and the site has a flat rate shipping of $4.95 (two business day shipping within the Continental U.S.). You can also get them on **Amazon** (www.amazon.com), **Lollicup** (www.lollicup.com) and a number of other online specialty coffee vendors.

Starbucks

Sugar-free Starbucks brand syrups are usually available at any Starbucks location simply by informing your barista that you would like to purchase a bottle.

My advice would be to start with the Torani and DaVinci websites, (www.torani.com and www.davinciusa.com respectively) but <u>not to order the syrups</u> (the prices at their sites is considerably higher than you can get elsewhere), but rather to look at all the sugar-free flavors available.

Sugar-free Concentrates/Powders/Mixes

Chai Tea Concentrate

The Chai Tea Concentrate can be especially hard to find. The only place I've been able to consistently find it is on the **DaVinci** website **(www.davinciusa.com).**

Green Tea Powder

You can get the green tea powder I suggested for the green tea smoothie from **Amazon** (www.amazon.com) or in most Asian grocery stores.

Peanut flour

Peanut flour is a product that is made when most of the oil is pressed from a peanut, leaving only a flour. Powdered peanut has approximately 85% less calories and fat than leading peanut butter, making it a great substitution for peanut butter in protein shakes. You can order it from **Amazon** or **Netrition.**

Sugar-free specialty drink mixes

For drinks like my protein piña colada you an use a variety of syrups and fruit. However, if you need a shake that is lower in carbohydrates or natural sugars, Baja Bob's drink mixes create the same effect for way less calories and carbs (not that fresh fruit is a bad thing but sometimes we have room for more in our day and sometimes we don't).

I've found two great places to get these mixes: Netrition (www.netrition.com) and BJ's Bariatrics (www.bjsbariatrics.com). Both will give you a good price and reasonable shipping.

Extracts

In several recipes I suggested extracts as an alternative to sugar-free syrups. Some extracts are easier to find than others. If you can't find an extract in your local grocery store, try a store that caters to cake makers or restaurant supply stores. And remember...a little extract goes a LONG way!

Made in the USA
San Bernardino, CA
13 May 2014